Speaking of Power
The Poetry of Di Brandt

Wilfrid Laurier University Press
www.wlupress.wlu.ca
75 University Avenue West, Waterloo, ON, N2L 3C5
Tel: 519-884-0710 ext. 2665, Fax: 519-725-1399
Toll-free: 866-836-5551, Email: press@wlu.ca

Speaking of Power: The Poetry of Di Brandt
Tanis MacDonald, editor • afterword by Di Brandt
$14.95 Paper, 72 pp. • ISBN: 0-88920-506-X • April 2006
Laurier Poetry series

We are pleased to send you this book for review. We would
appreciate receiving two copies of any review you might give
it.

For more information please contact Clare
Hitchens at 519-884-0710 ext. 2665,
clare@press.wlu.ca

Speaking of Power
The Poetry of Di Brandt

Selected
with an
introduction by
Tanis MacDonald
and an
afterword by
Di Brandt

LAURIER POETRY SERIES

Wilfrid Laurier University Press

We acknowledge the support of the Canada Council for the Arts for our publishing program. We acknowledge the financial support of the Government of Canada through the Book Publishing Industry Development Program for our publishing activities.

Library and Archives Canada Cataloguing in Publication

Brandt, Di

   Speaking of power : the poetry of Di Brandt / selected, with an introduction by Tanis MacDonald ; and an afterword by Di Brandt.

(Laurier poetry series)
Includes bibliographical references.
ISBN-13: 978-0-88920-506-2
ISBN-10: 0-88920-506-X

   I. MacDonald, Tanis, 1962–   II. Title.   III. Series.

PS8553.R2953A6 2006   c811'.54   C2006-901443-4

© 2006 Wilfrid Laurier University Press
Waterloo, Ontario, Canada N2L 3C5
www.wlupress.wlu.ca

Cover image: Joe Rosenblatt, *Ms. Nature and Her Pals* from *The Voluptuous Gardener* series, 1986. Mixed media drawing, watercolour, and ink, 11" × 4". Courtesy of the artist.

Cover and text design by P. J. Woodland.

Every reasonable effort has been made to acquire permission for copyright material used in this text, and to acknowledge all such indebtedness accurately. Any errors and omissions called to the publisher's attention will be corrected in future printings.

This book is printed on 100% post-consumer recycled paper.

Printed in Canada

Table of Contents

Foreword

At the beginning of the twenty-first century, poetry in Canada—writing and publishing it, reading and thinking about it—finds itself in a strangely conflicted place. We have many strong poets continuing to produce exciting new work, and there is still a small audience for poetry; but increasingly, poetry is becoming a vulnerable art, for reasons that don't need to be rehearsed.

But there are things to be done: we need more real engagement with our poets. There needs to be more access to their work in more venues—in classrooms, in the public arena, in the media—and there needs to be more, and more different kinds of publications, that make the wide range of our contemporary poetry more widely available.

The hope that animates this new series from Wilfrid Laurier University Press is that these volumes will help to create and sustain the larger readership that contemporary Canadian poetry so richly deserves. Like our fiction writers, our poets are much celebrated abroad; they should just as properly be better known at home.

Our idea has been to ask a critic (sometimes herself a poet) to select thirty-five poems from across a poet's career; write an engaging, accessible introduction; and have the poet write an afterword. In this way, we think that the usual practice of teaching a poet through eight or twelve poems from an anthology will be much improved upon; and readers in and out of classrooms will have more useful, engaging, and comprehensive introductions to a poet's work. Readers might also come to see more readily, we hope, the connections among, as well as the distances between, the life and the work.

It was the ending of an Al Purdy poem that gave Margaret Laurence the epigraph for *The Diviners*: "but they had their being once / and left a place to stand on." Our poets still do, and they are leaving many places to stand on. We hope that this series will help, variously, to show how and why this is so.

—*Neil Besner*
General Editor

Biographical Note

Di Brandt grew up in Reinland, a Mennonite farming village in south-central Manitoba and, with her first book, *questions i asked my mother* (1987), became one of the first women writers to break the public silence of Mennonite women in Canada. She has published four other collections of poetry: *Agnes in the sky* (1990); *mother, not mother* (1992); *Jerusalem, beloved* (1995); and *Now You Care* (2003). She has received the Canadian Authors Association National Poetry Award, the McNally Robinson Award for Manitoba Book of the Year, and the Gerald Lampert Award, and has been twice shortlisted for the Governor General's Award for Poetry, as well as for the Griffin Poetry Prize, Ontario's Trillium Book Award, and the Dillons Commonwealth Poetry Prize. She is a former poetry editor of *Prairie Fire* and a founding member of the feminist editorial collective of *Contemporary Verse 2*. She taught English and creative writing at the University of Winnipeg from 1986–1995, and at the University of Windsor from 1997–2005. She currently holds a Canada Research Chair in Literature and Creative Writing at Brandon University in Manitoba.

In addition to her poetic work, Brandt has published a critical study of contemporary Canadian women's texts, *Wild Mother Dancing: Maternal Narrative in Canadian Literature* (University of Manitoba Press, 1993), and a collection of essays on cross-cultural poetics, *Dancing Naked: Narrative Strategies for Writing across Centuries* (Mercury, 1996). She released *Awakenings*, a collaborative poetry/music CD featuring her own poetry and that of Dorothy Livesay, with music by Carol Ann Weaver and Rebecca Campbell, in 2003. *Re:Generations*, a multimedia poetry anthology, which Brandt co-edited with Barbara Godard, was released by Black Moss Press in 2006. Two more critical works, *This Land That I Love* (part of the Writer as Critic series from NeWest Press) and *Wider Boundaries of Daring: The Modernist Impulse in Canadian Women's Poetry* (also co-edited with Godard), are forthcoming.

Introduction

The importance of Di Brandt's poetry to Canadian literature cannot be over-estimated. Her work broaches complex and volatile subject matter, and is valued for her assertion that poetry must be, at its core, concerned with the political power of language. Acclaimed for her lyric sensibility and rebellious inquiry into the power of language, Brandt explores cross-cultural concepts of justice and the ecopoetic relationship between land and spirituality. Critical discussions of Brandt's poetry began with an examination of her influence on the profusion of Canadian Mennonite writing in the 1980s (Tiessen and Hinchcliffe, 1992), and subsequently, critics have focused upon her exploration of domestic violence (Boire, 1993), subversions of language (Kehler, 1995), maternity and power (Fisher, 1996), and her development of a feminist ethics (Carrière, 2002).

Brandt's stylistic and formal innovations distinguish her as part of a group of women writers that began working with feminist poetics in the 1980s, searching for ways to write the female body as a challenge to the patriarchal tradition of Western literature. Writing the poems for *questions i asked my mother*, Brandt discovered "a child's voice, breathless, hurried, scared" when advised by Maara Haas to remove punctuation from her poems (1993, 37). Brandt writes that the voice gave her a way to crack the silence of her childhood, forcing her to listen to the sound of her breath in order to discover the rhythm of the line (38). In his 1991 review of Brandt's second book, *Agnes in the sky*, Stephen Scobie offers an eloquent reading of her prosody, emphasizing that her "line breaks work at cross-purposes to the conversational rhythms, but they hold the poems in check; they enforce the sudden transitions and juxtapositions." He maintains that Brandt's poems "exist in this tension between outcry and control … which ensures their power, their importance and their beauty" (110). With *mother, not mother* (1992), Brandt searches for a more deliberate, less resonant narrative line, as she exchanges her long lines for the stringency of couplets. The resulting clipped rhythm, forced stops, and compressed poetic space create a voice that speaks of the paradox of motherhood in Western culture. The volume turns toward addressing the historical trauma of political forms of fear and divisiveness as the origin of family violence, extrapolated to the large structures of racism and sexism. In *Jerusalem, beloved* (1995), she composes snapshots of conflict and spirituality at the root of ancient cultures. Brandt's explorations of language, gender, and power expand to encompass global concerns while maintaining their specificity with the local and personal. In *Now You Care* (2003), she takes on a large public voice to claim a passionate ecopoetics that sings through an intertextual allusiveness, tying the future of the planet to the ecstatic, or destructive, power of the word.

With their arresting line breaks and demanding syntax, Brandt's poems have an insistent, oracular quality that pulls the reader into an inquiry about the power of speech in Western civilization. Although much of her poetry is intentionally disquieting, the disturbance Brandt creates is never gratuitous; for her, writing poetry means nothing less than discovering where the power in language is located. Politics, in Brandt's poetry, may be defined as a series of decisions about who has the privilege of speech and who does not— ultimately, who lives and who dies.

Grace Kehler discusses Brandt's poetic persona as a feminist version of the Aboriginal trickster, the "rebel traitor thief" of the opening poem in *questions i asked my mother*. This version of the trickster steals language in order to speak in a powerful poetic feminine discourse. The feminine, for Brandt, is located, first and foremost, in the maternal body, and is acted out in the relationship between mother and daughter, removed from the systems of filiation that dominate much of Western literature. Brandt has written extensively about the role of feminism and motherhood; her critical text, *Wild Mother Dancing* (1993), grew out of her dissertation on maternal narratives in Canadian literature. In a 1999 article in *West Coast Line*, Brandt quotes Métisse activist and writer Maria Campbell on the need to "put the mother back in the language," a literary strategy to escape the "old matricidal paradigm...the erasure of body, land, and mother from the social text" (101). The metaphor of stealing the language in order to "put the mother back" into it is of central importance to Brandt's poetry. When Magdalene Redekop writes on the back cover of *questions i asked my mother*, "Read these poems and you'll discover a Mennonite Eve stealing some breath for herself," she glosses Brandt's quest to be an attentive thief of language in order to find some poetic space for women's bodies. Much of Brandt's work responds to traditions that have organized literary, cultural, or spiritual thought: the Bible, Mennonite culture, gender construction, and the complexities of motherhood.

A closer look at Brandt's poetry highlights the struggles and successes of her inquiry into language and power. Even as she writes eloquently about beauty and the need for spiritual integrity ("when I was five," "prairie hymn"), Brandt questions the authority of doctrinal religious faith as an oppressive tool of patriarchy, personified as a father figure. In "but what do you think my father says," the daughter argues against her father's oppressive religious devotion, emphasizing that gendered language denies power to women. Brandt offers an agonized declaration of hypocrisy in "nonresistance, or love Mennonite style," pointing out that the theological conscientious objection against armed conflict is contradicted by the domestic violence of that closed community. Brandt shows the mother's problematic complicity in this belief system, obeying the father's commands even as "her / body is shouting No! No!" This tension between men and women, between command and defiance, between violence and love, thrives upon the silence that surrounds it, and Brandt asserts that the price exacted for silence is profoundly painful. In "mother why didn't you tell me this," the daughter confronts her mother with the corporeal crisis of womanhood, when "the body's great emptiness" becomes "unreadable," but remains inescapable.

The tone of this inquiry becomes more rebellious in poems that address female sexuality: the breathless "say to yourself each time" and the wickedly wry "missionary positions." The former poem explicitly evokes the female body, imitating the Renaissance blazon in the way that it "atomizes" the body, but subverting the tradition to reclaim female sexual selfhood. The six-part "missionary positions" series puns on sexual positions and spiritual attitudes to critique institutional suppression of female sexuality. With wit and audacity, Brandt rewrites biblical narrative in order to "revision," in Adrienne Rich's sense of the term, the possibilities of joyful female sexuality, and to recover the ecstatic spirituality of the erotic.

Such possibilities are important to recall when reading the intense struggle with patriarchy performed in these poems. The death of the father allows the daughter figure a way to separate the personal father from the patriarchal structure, though his death does not end the struggle between the daughter and patriarchal language. In a poem as marked by its despair as by its defiance, "today i spit out God & Jesus," Brandt presents a cautionary tale about striving after simplistic solutions to complex problems. Though admitting "death is a good argument," Brandt asserts that the removal of a single oppressive element does not guarantee the deconstruction of the larger belief system. The father figure begins as a personification of patriarchy, but after death, he does not become the grandiose and omniscient Lacanian "dead Father" (1977, 199), but rather, turns into a benevolent spirit of the land. In "& it amuses us to think," the daughters note that the dead father is "becoming one of us"; death has not reconfigured him into a vengeful Gothic ghost, but, rather, into a spirit freed from fear and rigidity. In "since we cannot meet on father ground," the daughter figure links her father's spirit to a legacy of community rather than ownership. By imagining "a new country" in place of "father ground," where men and women may "lay down … old weapons," Brandt invites readers to witness "the great / wooden door … creaking open at / last," a hope for a new, more inclusive kind of human knowledge. So, too, the ode-like "prairie hymn," with its "huge narrative / of the river the curved cry of the land," refigures the Christian "gathering at the river" into a narrative full of potential in the "words spoken / & unspoken between us."

The rebellion at the core of Brandt's work is both personally wrought and politically positioned, a ferocious attempt to clear the way for a more mater-nally inflected space. Such rebellion is frequently playful or subversively witty, and Brandt acknowledges that rebellion may, paradoxically, clear the way for reparation. In "my mother found herself one late summer" and "you prepare a banquet in your mind," Brandt writes the mother figure as part of a large earthy community, situating strength of maternal love as a force to be respected, honoured with ceremony, and blessed with attention. These poems speak of a daughter's hope for an expressive and expansive sense of woman-hood, while attempting to bridge the unspoken tension between her mother and herself. The daughter reclaims the mother through recuperating the trust and joy in their relationship, a trust that she seeks to maintain with her own daughters.

The pregnant body becomes a third site of reparation in Brandt's poetry, as her search for spiritual integrity blossoms into a celebration of maternal consciousness. Far from suggesting that such a revelation comes easily, Brandt emphasizes that her desire to write the strength and beauty of the regenerative female body is hampered by the fact that the maternal image is, at once, sym-bolically central and culturally peripheral in Western culture, something she discusses in greater detail in *Wild Mother Dancing*. While "let me tell you, dear reader" reimagines the pregnant body as a ship with "sails billowing, / full of wind, spirit breath, / baby's breath," and the poem "completely seduced" suggests that motherhood makes the woman "a goddess, the source, / the very planet" in the eyes of her baby, the maternal body remains "ordinary," neither annihilated by exhaustion nor exalted by procreation. The tension of existing as "half mother, / half not mother" presages the tension between reality and idealism in Brandt's poem for "a guy who's / thought about feminism," and her elegy for the women killed in the Montreal Massacre, "the letters I wrote & didn't." Both poems suggest that the political exigencies of feminism scrape against the reality of heterosexual relationships, in which "what you don't want / to know can hurt you, // & will," a fear that men and women "must greet / each other from now on // with lies or terror."

Intriguing tensions in Brandt's work grow from her sensitivity to the complexities of identity politics, particularly her sense of a "double identity" that becomes a problem of reference complicated by the limits of language (1993, 37). In "why she can't write *the mother*," Brandt captures the frustration of finding the word "*mother*" inadequate to describe the effort of nurturing "the goddamn fucking world." Brandt consistently challenges the assumption that the world is aligned along an immutable set of binaries, and suggests instead that even though the material and cultural conditions of a life may appear to be deeply contradictory, they do constitute a lived reality that must be acknowledged. The articulation of such double identities is part of Brandt's effort to speak against silence. In probing the ways that language may represent both oppression and freedom, she emphasizes the inherent difficulties of language and reference. In writing about "what *de Englische* / didn't understand," Brandt rejects the idea that assuming a feminist stance is an instant remedy for an unequal power dynamic. Brandt makes it clear that leaving the Mennonite community was not the answer to gaining freedom from language, and that the relative freedoms that non-Mennonites enjoy free them neither from their own servitude to language nor from responsibility for their history as oppressors of Mennonite, Jewish, and Aboriginal peoples.

In *Jerusalem, beloved,* Brandt's view of the terrible beauty of the Middle-Eastern desert pushes the debate about the dangers of defining land as commodity into an international arena. Recording the shattering political tensions of life in the Middle East, Brandt contrasts the Christian concept of Jerusalem as the site of spiritual love with its geographical realities of violent conflict. Re-examining the poetic relationship between land and motherhood in "there are no words in me for Gaza," "how long does it take to forget a murder," and "how badly she wants peace," Brandt returns to the double identity to explore the contradictory realities of talking about peace in a war zone. In "here, in the desert," she concentrates upon an ancient landscape of spiritual and sacred combat in which "history is undone" and "temptation is everything, because the Word means / nothing, is emptied out." Story, in this poem, is "crumbling" into desert sand, even as it is being rewritten.

In *Now You Care*, Brandt's ecopoetic poems of "passionate accusation" (Nurse 2004, 18) frame the power struggles of the earlier books, indicting the abuse of language as the core of destructive power. Focusing on the capitalist commodification of landscapes in southwestern Ontario and Eastern Europe, Brandt positions the land as urgently alive and desperately threatened. She breaks down the Romantic conventions of landscape poetry to contrast the literary construction of a pastoral idyll against the harsh chemical reality of a poisoned environment. In "Zone: < le Détroit >," her speaker imagines a chemical or nuclear crisis that devastates the earth and all human life, sparing only the speaker and her companion to experience a devastating isolation. For Brandt, the earth is the connective tissue between all forms of life, the bedrock of compassionate consciousness. Her ecopoetic verse acknowledges the annihilation of the natural world, and points to corporate greed as the agent of destruction.

In "Dog days in Maribor," a sequence of twelve "Anti (electric) ghazals," Brandt honours the use of the ghazal form in Canadian poetry as an articulation of despair, particularly as the form has been used in John Thompson's "Stilt Jack" (1973–76), and Phyllis Webb's "Sunday Water: Thirteen Anti Ghazals" (1982). Thompson describes the ghazal form as "the poem of contrasts, dreams, astonishing leaps" that produces "a chart of the disorderly" while discovering its revelatory design (1995, 106). Energized by what Brandt calls "the threat of encroaching technologies on creaturely tenderness," her ghazals have "an electric thread running through them" (2003, 123) that targets the global environmental situation as a crisis in consciousness. Brandt invokes the history of poetry, as well as her own history as a poet, to compress images of a dying planet into a refigured poetic tradition. Echoes of Shakespeare, Yeats, Baudelaire, Eliot, Rilke, Plath, cummings, and Williams "dog" these ghazals, as Brandt refashions the declarative statements of poetic predecessors to comment on the failing health of women, animals, rivers, and plants. Brandt's subversion of Yeats's opening words of "Sailing to Byzantium" to "That is no country for old women" supports her savage irony on the necessity for "more mastectomies, / cut them all off!" The trickster-thief is back, once again stealing in order to speak. How can the mother return to the language when the generative ability of the planet has been poisoned by structures of corporeal and semantic violence? Brandt's interest in shamanic models of transformation that value the earth and seek to maintain its natural gifts offers a vision of ecstatic renewal in the midst of technological despair.

Writing at the intersections of gender, power, and language, Brandt calls poetry "a way of listening ... an act of survival & transformation in a world that's currently in jeopardy" (1993, 40). She concentrates on the way complex circumstances or conditions of power (politics, religion, corporatism) frequently rely upon a single set of assumptions that negate the value of certain forms of life, even to the point of death. Demonstrating a willingness to "let the silence speak" (Brandt 1996, 18) as a critique of institutions that perpetuate oppression, Brandt's inquiry has grown into an urgent discussion about the future of the planet, wrought through her concern with the corporate, and often corporeal, abuse of power. Her ethics of interconnection emphasize that no action or word can exist in brutal isolation or untouchable transcendence, and assert that the fabric of individual existence is deeply interdependent upon all forms of life on earth. Brandt's concept of her "double identity," as poet and critic, as Mennonite and feminist, as mother and daughter, performs its own interconnections, and grants her access to a grand vision of beauty and regenerative hope. Brandt's work is best read as a lyrical arc rather than individual poems, for each of her concerns resonates with an adjoining issue: feminism with religion; power with gender; ecology with corporatism. The poems selected for this collection emphasize the connections between people, between love and loss, between anger and grief, between personal account-ability and collective adversity. By clarifying these complexities without sim-plifying them, Brandt's poetry sings with a voice that is pressured by desperate circumstances but predicates a better world with its ecstatic music.

—*Tanis MacDonald*

Bibliography

Boire, Gary. 1993. "Transparencies: Of Sexual Abuse, Ambivalence, and Resistance." *Essays on Canadian Writing* 51–52: 211–233.

Brandt, Di. 1990. *Agnes in the sky.* Winnipeg, MB: Turnstone.

———. 1996. *Dancing Naked: Narrative Strategies for Writing Across Centuries.* Toronto: Mercury.

———. 1993. "Interrogating Language: The Writing Act." *Prairie Fire* 13.4: 37–40.

———. 1995. *Jerusalem, beloved.* Winnipeg, MB: Turnstone.

———. 1992. *mother, not mother.* Toronto: Mercury.

———. 2003. *Now You Care.* Toronto: Coach House.

———. 1987. *questions i asked my mother.* Winnipeg, MB: Turnstone.

———. 2003. "Post-Slovenian Reflections: Anti ghazals, with an electric thread." *The New Quarterly* 85: 122–23.

———. 1999. "Putting the Mother Back in the Language: Maria Campbell's Revisionary Biogeographies & Margaret Laurence's *The Diviners.*" *West Coast Line* 29.33: 86–105.

———. 1993. *Wild Mother Dancing: Maternal Narrative in Canadian Literature.* Winnipeg, MB: University of Manitoba Press.

Carrière, Marie. 2002. *Writing in the Feminine in French and English Canada: A Question of Ethics.* Toronto: University of Toronto Press.

Fisher, Sheldon. 1996. "Mother, Me, My Daughter: Feminism, *Maternité*, and the Poetry of Di Brandt." *Wascana Review* 31.1: 31–48.

Kehler, Grace. 1995. "Stealing the Word(s): The Subversion of Monologic Language in Di Brandt's *Questions i asked my mother.*" *Open Letter* 9.2: 19–28.

Lacan, Jacques. 1977. *Écrits: A Selection.* Translated by Alan Sheridan. London, UK: Tavistock.

Nurse, Donna Bailey. 2004. "Di Brandt: Poems of Passionate Accusation." *Quill & Quire* 70.6: 18–19.

Rich, Adrienne. 1979. "When We Dead Awaken: Writing as Revision." *On Lies, Secrets, and Silence: Selected Prose, 1966–1978*. New York: W.W. Norton. 33–49.

Scobie, Stephen. 1991. Review of *Agnes in the sky. Malahat Review* 94: 110.

Thompson, John. 1995. *Collected Poems and Translations*, edited by Peter Sanger. Fredericton, NB: Goose Lane.

Tiessen, Hildi Froese, and Peter Hinchcliffe, eds. 1992. *Acts of Concealment: Mennonite/s Writing in Canada*. Waterloo, ON: University of Waterloo Press.

Webb, Phyllis. 1982. *Sunday Water: Thirteen Anti Ghazals*. Lantzville, BC: Island Writing.

※

when i was five i thought heaven was located
in the hayloft of our barn the ladder to get
up there was straight & narrow like the Bible
said if you fell off you might land on the
horns of a cow or be smashed on cement the men
in the family could leap up in seconds wielding
pitchforks my mother never even tried for us
children it was hard labour i was the scaredy
i couldn't reach the first rung so i stood at
the bottom & imagined what heaven was like there
was my grandfather with his Santa Claus beard
sitting on a wooden throne among straw bales
never saying a word but smiling & patting us
on the head & handing out bubble gum to those
who were good even though his eyes were half
closed he could see right inside your head so
i squirmed my way to the back of the line &
unwished the little white lie i had told which
i could feel growing grimy up there & tried
not to look at the dark gaping hole where they
shoved out black sinners like me but the best
part was the smell of new pitched hay wafting
about some of it fell to where i stood under
the ladder there were tiny blue flowerets pressed
on dry stems i held them to my nose & breathed
deep sky & sun it was enough heaven for me for
one day

※

but what do you think my father says this verse means if it's not
about the end of the world look that's obviously a misreading i say
the verb grammatically speaking doesn't have an object in this
instance so it can't possibly be made to that's exactly what i mean
he says waving the book in mid air if my father ever shouted he
would be shouting now you don't really care about the meaning all
you ever think about is grammar & fancy words i never even heard of
where i come from the reason you learn to read is to understand God's
Holy Word i only went to school 7 year & it's done me okay what are
you going to do with all this hifalutin education anyway don't you
think it's time you got a job & did some honest work for a change
the meaning i say through clenched teeth is related to the structure
of the sentence for godsake anybody can see that you can't just take
some old crackpot idea & say you found it in these words even the
Bible has to make some sense the Bible my father says the veins in
his neck turning a slow purple is revealed to those gathered together
in His name you don't even go to church how can you know anything of
the truth you're no better than the heathen on the street the way
you live around here if i'd aknown my own daughter would end up like
this you're the one i say who started this conversation what did you
ask me for if i'm not entitled to an opinion please my mother says
crying as usual why don't we go for a walk or something you think
i'll weep i'll not weep we glare at each other with bright fierce
eyes my father & i she still tries after all these years to end this
argument between us arrest deflect its bitter motion does she know
this is all there is for us these words dancing painfully across the
sharp etched lines of his God ridden book & does she does he do we
really want this crazy cakewalk to stop

※

say to yourself each time lips vagina tongue
lips do not exist catch the rising sob in
your throat where it starts deep under your
belly the tips of your breasts your secret
flowing your fierce wanting & knowing say
to yourself the ache in your thighs your big
head full of lies your great empty nothing
despise despise the Word of God is the Word
of God sit still stop your breathing look
down at your numb legs your false skirt sighing
sit still & listen

※

my mother found herself one late summer
afternoon lying in grass under the wild
yellow plum tree jewelled with sunlight
she was forgotten there in spring picking
rhubarb for pie & the children home from
school hungry & her new dress half hemmed
for Sunday the wind & rain made her skin
ruddy like a peach her hair was covered
with wet fallen crab apple blossoms she
didn't know what to do with her so she put
her up in the pantry among glass jars of
jellied fruit she might have stayed there
all winter except we were playing robbers
& the pantry was jail & every caught thief
of us heard her soft moan she made her
escape while we argued over who broke the
pickled watermelon jar scattering cubes
of pale pink flesh in vinegar over the
basement floor my mother didn't mind she
handed us mop & broom smiling & went back
upstairs i think she was listening to
herself in the wind singing

missionary position (1)

let me tell you what it's like
having God for a father & jesus
for a lover on this old mother
earth you who no longer know
the old story the part about the
Virgin being of course a myth
made up by Catholics for an easy
way out it's not that easy i can
tell you right off the old man
in his room demands bloody hard
work he with his rod & his hard
crooked staff well jesus he's
different he's a good enough lay
it's just that he prefers miracles
to fishing & sometimes i get tired
waiting all day for his bit of
magic though late at night i burn
with his fire & the old mother
shudders & quakes under us when
God's not looking

missionary position (5)

of all the virgins that last summer
heidi you & i we were the wisest
how we strutted down empty streets
lamps nearly bursting not spilling
a drop how we dreamed of our bride
groom the shadowy prince disdaining
boys' touches oh we knew what we
wanted not for us to be caught with
our pants down & oil running out
not with heaven beckoning us no sir
how we smirked at the foolish ones
burning their capital after dark
behind closed shops how we gloated
over our own saving we waited wise
virgins that long summer to be swept
into clouds we wandered fires unlit
to its end

※

mother why didn't you tell me this
how everything in the middle of life
becomes its opposite & all the signs
turn unreadable every direction a
dead end why didn't you tell me about
the belly's trembling just when you
need strength how the brain turns to
mush when it most needs to be clear
when you promised us passion & warned
us about boys why didn't you tell
about the body's great emptiness its
wanting the void the tight ache of
heart's muscle in the middle of night
the shaking of knees

※

you prepare a banquet in your mind
for your mother & the man who shared
your grief in the night & the woman
who saved your life & your beautiful
daughters you gather wildflowers to
put at their places fireweed foxtail
goldenrod you collect acorns you paint
the table you hang ribbons from the
trees you order sweet nectar you leave
a place for the stranger you write to
your sister you inscribe the invitations
in green ink festooned with garlands
you scatter the ground with ash seeds
you imagine a feast you prepare a
banquet in your mind for your mother

※

since we cannot meet on father ground
our father's land as sister & brother ever
let's imagine a new place between us
slightly suspended in air but yet touching
earth an old tree house full of weather
or an ark its ancient hull gleaming
remembering the rains let's gather our
belongings & our children & meet at the
river this will be a new country love &
crossing the field to greet you i will lay
my old weapons down & wait if you are
there with me under the harvest moon
we will look in each other's eyes without
speaking our hands will shake & the great
wooden door will begin creaking open at
last since we cannot meet

nonresistance, or love Mennonite style

turn the other cheek when your brother
hits you & your best friend tells fibs
about you & the teacher punishes you
unfairly if someone steals your shirt
give him your coat to boot this will
heap coals of fire on his head & let him
know how greatly superior you are
while he & his cronies dicker & bargain
their way to hell you can hold your
head up that is down humbly knowing
you're bound for the better place where
it gets tricky is when your grandfather
tickles you too hard or your cousins
want to play doctor & your uncle kisses
you too long on the lips & part of you
wants it & the other part knows it's
wrong & you want to run away but you
can't because he's a man like your father
& the secret place inside you feels itchy
& hot & you wonder if this is what hell
feels like & you remember the look on
your mother's face when she makes
herself obey your dad & meanwhile her
body is shouting *No! No!* & he doesn't
even notice & you wish you could stop
being angry all the time but you can't
because God is watching & he sees
everything there isn't any place to let
it out & you understand about love the
lavish sacrifice in it how it will stretch
your woman's belly & heap fire on your
head you understand how love is like
a knife & a daughter is not a son & the

only way you will be saved is by
submitting quietly in your grandfather's
house your flesh smouldering in the
darkened room as you love your enemy
deeply unwillingly & full of shame

prairie hymn

what i want is the shape of the story of the blood
jolting seasonally to & from the heart underneath
the small gestures of our hands the words spoken
& unspoken between us i want the huge narrative
of the river the curved cry of the land i want the
straight blowing of birch leaves in strong wind
the whistling of prairie grass your lit face in the
distance coming to meet me your arms hot like
August prairie sky all around me

※

why she can't write *the mother*,
though she has birthed two children,

spends half her day feeding clothing
sheltering them,

picking up dirty rolled up socks
cooking macaroni,

though she has stretched herself thin,
scarred skin over bloated belly,

watched leftover blood shoot clotted
like fists from her emptied womb,

though she's exhausted herself, black
& blue, many times

mothering the goddamn fucking world

why she can't write herself around
that,

why she can't put down simply,
i am the mother,

& leave it like that

✳

let me tell you, dear reader,
about the time

my body was a ship. & i
sailed the seas

of downtown Toronto in it,
sails billowing,

full of wind, spirit breath,
baby's breath.

& the young men on Bloor
averted their eyes

& the Portuguese construction
workers on Huron Street

whistled through their teeth
& grunted,

ah, now, there's a mama.

& the young women in the park
coming suddenly into view,

with their strollers on the green
grass, & i sailing

down the sidewalks past them,
glorious in my pride.

ah, dear reader, let me tell you
how i loved my body then,

my huge floating belly, my nipples
big, dark, swollen

with milk, leaking desire,
golden, liquid,

all over the bed & the pillow
& the floor.

ah, how i loved my lover then,
who filled me with such bounty,

erotic trembling, oceanic bliss.

smacking, sucking, stroking
my sunlit prow, big with child.

it was then, dear reader,
my brain sank into my womb,

dark lipped, bearded, dripping:
with child, with child, with child.

such a grand billowing
on the high seas, such unfurling,

such a mighty flowering among
the busy streets,

expecting, pregnant.

※

completely seduced
by motherhood,

this is how you got
through the day.

without sleep,
without pay,

without help,
words,

companions,
a break.

your mind bouncing
off walls,

& the ceiling
& the floor,

eyes blurred
with exhaustion.

you weren't thinking
about that.

you weren't thinking
about your stretched

skin.

you saw yourself
in the dark pool

of your baby's eyes,
shining,

a goddess, the source,
the very planet.

your breaths flowing
together,

your breasts filled
with milk & honey.

all night, you were
the earth,

rocking.

(later, you shrank
into an ordinary

middle-aged woman,
enjoying sleep.

amused by the ordinary
world,

half mother,
half not mother.

bewildered by time
& place,

& wrinkled skin.
& missing children.)

※

what *de Englische*
didn't understand:

that telling my story
didn't make me one of them.

that my fear of being silenced
isn't obsolete.

i came from far away,
& brought everything with me.

the body remembers being
beaten & tortured & killed.

i stole the language
of their kings & queens,

but i didn't bow down to it,
i didn't become a citizen.

how hard it is to tell a story
so it can be heard.

how easily the reader climbs
on top of it,

pronouncing judgment,
the eternal optimist, tourist,

pointing fingers.

it wasn't about being Mennonite,
(or Indian or Jew).

it was about you, you.

how glad i am to be a human
being & not a Wasp.

is this about gender or isn't it?

oceans are dying & here we sit
discussing words.

the roaring in your ears,
the whale inside you: listen.

how much you wanted to cry
in the night but couldn't.

how deeply the body carries
its violence, well hidden,

afraid of its own speaking.

say it slowly, each syllable,
out loud:

MMMMMMMMMMMMMM
AAAAAAAAAAAAAAAAAA
MMMMMMMMMMMMMM
EEEEEEEEEEEEEEEEEEEE
MMMMMMMMMMMMMM
AAAAAAAAAAAAAAAAAA
MMMMMMMMMMMMMM
EEEEEEEEEEEEEEEEEEEE
MMMMMMMMMMMMMM
AAAAAAAAAAAAAAAAAA
AAAAAAAAAHHHHHHHHH

how much you needed her,
through the centuries,

the here & now.

what kind of reaching out,
what kind of holding,

what kind of touch between us,
listener:

between the hiss of consonants,
the inner wail, the heart

beating its old music, deep,
& hot, & unforgiving.

※

the letters i wrote & didn't
send,

the letters i didn't write,
in November,

dry, without snow,
clear-eyed, into winter,

alone, not alone.

angel, on my right side,
tell me, who

among the millions
will hear me, crying

at night, who'll read
what i can't write,

against the tide,
the sea that is dying.

a world full
of ex-soldiers,

& failed heroes,
& impotent men.

o my sisters.
if you love this planet.

how i have needed you,
mother.

if i ride the waves,
this time,

not looking back,
to the sea women,

if i carry
the unspoken stories,

like babies, screaming,
scars on my skin,

oh beautiful ones,
will you read me,

trace your fingers
across my back,

my salt wounds,
my old longing,

wrapped in seaweed,
flotsam,

the great underwater
tow

knowing the dark
intimately

you

(Written December 6, 1989, & dedicated to the memory of Geneviève, Hélène, Nathalie, Barbara, Annie, Anne-Marie, Maud, Annie, Maryse, Anne-Marie, Maryse, Sonia, Barbara Maria, Michèle, of Montreal.)

※

poem for a guy who's
thought about feminism

& is troubled by it,
but not enough:

what you don't want
to know can hurt you,

& will, perhaps even
kill you, as it has killed

so many others, women,
whales, birds, Indians,

Jews, even the golden-
haired sons of men,

the privileged ones,
the chosen.

why do we hide grief
from ourselves,

& each other, pretending
pleasure? i cry

because we must greet
each other from now on

with lies or terror,
our lying together

through the years
has brought us

to such an impasse,
such a possible ending,

i fear we must,
all of us,

everything in us,
fly apart.

i feel a heaviness in me
tonight, the earth's

weight pulling me,
down. i want to love

you, under these dripping
trees, these great

scented blossoms,
but i can't.

enchanted evening,
you would have liked

to whisper in my ear,
in another language,

another story, your
heart in your throat.

the poem is bigger
than i am. the poem

is hungry, & insists
on its own truth.

the desire in every
thing, fierce

breeding among the trees.
i love you, i love you.

i cannot lie, i cannot lie
with you tonight,

there's holocaust
between us,

& i'm tired of dying.

※

death is a good argument.
better than fathers,

better than God.
better than any of

the twisted reasons
you gave me,

in my face, my arms,
bones, shiners,

lighting us together
into the night.

better than the entire
library of Western

thought, better than
promises, flowers,

panting, gold.

once you know it,
you are never lonely,

& only marginally
afraid.

you hold it deep inside
you, at the centre,

where you begin
& end. everything else

is relative.
sometimes i forget,

i long again
for the old pain,

the fist in the face,
the twisted twirly

fate, the bitter taste
of absence

on the tongue, you.

i admit i have cried
at night for my father

& his Word,
the old terrible God.

i have listened
under the old sobbing,

to flesh singing,
earth pushing its way

through the debris,
even now,

under the weight
of so much garbage,

diseased cells,
darkly into sun.

in the stillness
at the heart of things,

under the thump
of blood,

past the long reach
of the Old Story,

where the dream is,
the nothing in us,

full of fire.

※

today i spit out God & Jesus
for the last time.

mary mother mary,
how i wish this were true.

how sick i am of these
pieces of Godhead

sticking in my throat.
how my bowels ache

with Godshit, the memory
of it, red muscles

contracting around emptiness,
crying for food.

i needed milk, i needed
your white hot breast

pressed against my mouth,
a woman's arms around

my head.
the tree in my bedroom

has been sprouting leaves,
the vines on my sheets

are bearing fruit,
blossoms, grapes, wine,

flowing like blood
all over the room.

the branches outside
my window cast shadows

against the church,
intricate lace patterns

against the brick.
the hobo walks by, smiling

at his new boots.
(the world on fire,

& us huddled in old
dreams, feeling

the earth shudder
against our feet,

our eyes open
a brief second:

the knife slashing air,
the world thunder

※

& it amuses us to think that in death you're becoming
one of us, fond of ritual, & superstition, a regular old
ghost, speaking with us the language of tobacco, &
magic rings & crystal, & bits of cloth hung on trees,
on a wild riverbank, beside an old haunted graveyard,
with a bunch of crying, laughing women, how you
would have scoffed at us in life, for dabbling in
spirits, & feelings, & dreams, afraid of their power,
how temporary after all is that mighty world system
you believed in so much, unable to take you into
death, into the black night, unable to sustain you in
joy longer than it takes to count up the profits, the
harvest, next summer's grain prices, to tally up the
many, contradictory Words of God, & oh daddy,
isn't this fun, now that you're spirit & we're grown
women, wild spirited, like you, here beside this
brown river, in tall grass, lying among weeds, under
willows & sugar maples, drunk with wild blossom
scented sun, & prairie sky, & women's laughter, feet
in the air

※

Jerusalem, the golden, city of my dreams,
dreaming, how i waited all my life for you,
to find you, resplendent, in the sun, your
white stones crying, with joy, Jerusalem,
beloved, lying in the Mediterranean sun,
filled with love, delirious with love, *lift up
your heart & sing*, my heart dancing, how i
longed for you, all my life, your streets
paved with gold, & children playing, your
diamond studded gates, your rooftops filled
with women, dancing, & flowers in their
hair, the tables laden, heavy, the air filled
with music, & feasting, my love, how i
longed for you, dreaming, my arms aching,
from the day of my birth, my birthgiving,
filled with pangs of hunger & remembering,
how i longed for you, my love, how long,
oh how long i waited for you

※

there are no words in me for Gaza, for what i saw
in Gaza, the eyes of the women lining up at the
hospital for milk, with their babies & small
children, their eyes looking at me, another North
American tourist with nothing to offer, except
terrible pity, & shame, shame at my innocence,
my stupid privilege, i never imagined such a place,
i could have been born here, & thought this is what
the world is like, these narrow streets filled with
flies & cowdung, shacks made of sheet metal &
bare wooden boards, the path to the beach littered
with barbed wire & abandoned jeeps, & grey sand,
how long does it take to forget, the soldiers at the
door, the women screaming, the broken china,
embroidered tablecloths flapping in the wind,
blood running from the father's mouth, how long
does it take to forget, the darkness in this woman's
eyes, the children hiding rocks in their hands on
the way to school, these two will not come home
tonight, their shins broken by soldiers in the street,
these eyes, the long long sorrow in them, these
women's eyes, looking at me

※

how long does it take to forget a murder in your
house, behind a closed door, without a sound, no
words said, the hanging in a field your great
grandmother watched as a little girl, her face pushed
against her father's sleeve, a heretic slow burning at
the end of August in the town square? how long
does the body remember the bullet, where it graced
the flesh, the cells burned, blue black, where it
entered skin, nerve endings charred, trembling?
how long does it take to forget a gas chamber filled
with naked, terrified, bearded men, the roomful
of women, the accused, sentenced to burning, a
soldier's rifle under the chin, cocked, the soldier's
hand, shaking, full of hatred, shame, rage?

this black ball we carry around inside us, this
darkness, this red flaming sea, how it comes back
to us, this violence, to haunt us, a ghost, the devil, the
enemy, how it yearns, like tree roots, to take hold, to
flower in us, like branches & leaves:

the body's humiliation, trembling, how it stays in
the air, long after the body is gone, dismembered, the
spirit seeking revenge—or is it comforting it wants,
remembering, shaking, grieving, so we will not do it
again, to someone else, the way it was done to us, so
that the flowering can be trembling, beautiful, wise,
as newborn children are, instead of wrath?

※

here, in the desert, where everything comes together,
& history is undone, time rolls up into old scrolls,
bits of parchment, brittle, scattering in wind, stories
crumble like walls into sand, silence, old stones, bits
of bones, gritty against your feet, here where
temptation is everything, because the Word means
nothing, is emptied out, the heart listens to itself,
crying, the foxes in the desert have holes, the birds
in the air have nests.

Kathy says, don't let the children out of sight, there
have been kidnappings, settlers on the West Bank,
my stomach screaming briefly its old scream, &,
here they are, blond & brown hair gleaming, in the
sun, with their cameras & sandals, laughing, teasing,
my daughters, they've found a cave with two arched
doorways, black, just big enough to sit in, take a
picture of us, mom, see, they say, laughing, these are
our houses, *smile*.

※

how badly she wants peace, this wise woman, this
zionist, crone, how she cries out for it, her arms
stretching out across this jagged green line, black
lines laid down, over stone, to make a place, mark
home, in this holy city, these heavenly streets, baring
her breasts in the line of fire, between these walls of
fighting men, she will not give up her dream of
Jerusalem, she will not leave, she will not close her
eyes to the pain running through each pair of dark
eyes, meeting hers in the market, the taxi, at her
apartment gate, this land that is hers, and theirs,
and ours, this land of Ishmael & Isaac, this ancient singing
land, of Asherah, that cannot be conquered or sold,
groaning to be delivered, of its love child, its
afterthought, its illegitimate offspring, sudden
tenderness in the fields of war, she holds it to her
bosom, hungrily, there, there, i have enough milk
for you, *suck*

Zone : < le Détroit >
after Stan Douglas

1

Breathing yellow air
here, at the heart of the dream
of the new world,
the bones of old horses and dead Indians
and lush virgin land, dripping with fruit
and the promise of wheat,
overlaid with glass and steel
and the dream of speed:
all these our bodies
crushed to appease
the 400 & 1 gods
of the Superhighway,
NAFTA, we worship you,
hallowed be your name,
here, where we are scattered
like dust or rain in ditches,
the ghosts of passenger pigeons
clouding the silver towered sky,
the future clogged in the arteries
of the potholed city,
Tecumseh, come back to us
from your green grave,
sing us your song of bravery
on the lit bridge over the black river,
splayed with grief over the loss
of its ancient rainbow coloured
fish swollen joy.
Who shall be fisher king
over this poisoned country,
whose borders have become

a mockery,
blowing the world to bits
with cars and cars and trucks and electricity and cars,
who will cover our splintered
bones with earth and blood,
who will sing us back into—

Zone : < le Détroit >

2

See how there's no one going to Windsor,
only everyone coming from?
Maybe they've been evacuated,
maybe there's nuclear war,
maybe when we get there we'll be the only ones.
See all those trucks coming towards us,
why else would there be rush hour on the 401
on a Thursday at nine o'clock in the evening?
I counted 200 trucks and 300 cars
and that's just since London.
See that strange light in the sky over Detroit,
see how dark it is over Windsor?
You know how people keep disappearing,
you know all those babies born with deformities,
you know how organ thieves follow tourists
on the highway and grab them at night
on the motel turnoffs,
you know they're staging those big highway accidents
to increase the number of organ donors?
My brother knew one of the guys paid to do it,
$100,000 for twenty bodies
but only if the livers are good.
See that car that's been following us for the last hour,
see the pink glow of its headlights in the mirror?
That's how you know.
Maybe we should turn around,
maybe we should duck so they can't see us,
maybe it's too late,
maybe we're already dead,
maybe the war is over,
maybe we're the only ones alive.

※

Here at the heart of the ravaged heart
of the Dead Land, lilacs mixing with
the dead rain, we like to kill our gods
and eat them too, like all good christians
do, no mystery moths or beetles for us,
or locusts shining in the grass, nosiree,
all our trillion little winged deities, bees,
mosquitoes, houseflies, butterflies,
fruitflies, fishflies, horseflies, Junebugs,
cicadas now in radical chemical jeopardy,
and our lettuce and raspberries, and yet,
and yet, deer graze in the forest along
the ravine, grasshoppers and crickets
miraculously sing in forgotten ditches
along the fields, wasps stray through
chlorpyrifos clouds to out of the way
sweet milkweed, thistle, goldenrod
clumps, just then for a moment, above
around below the shadow of the shadow
of these endless depleted uranium driven
grey grey grey grey grey apocalyptic
streets, these lurking cancer cells, hawks
and goldfinches, bright coloured, let's
turn it all around, asphalt splitting
volcanic magic, blue butterflies, sweet
grass, adrenalin, circling darting
fluttering kicking bursting in

Dog days in Maribor: Anti (electric) ghazals

1   Truly, in this age,
why should not all women be mad?

The snapping turtle stares
at the giant ball of rope in the sky.

The cherry trees have all been cut;
bronzed epitaphs.

No more invasions!
The earth is spitting up blood.

Diamond rivers, uranium valleys,
petroleum oceans.

Purple irises, Van Gogh, radiant,
beside the door.

2   These days it is the dogs, gold hearted,
who must teach us.

We are spinning in space
in the key of C# minor.

Or spiders, dizzy, drunk,
flying out over the river Esk.

Who shall console us,
with the belly dancers on strike?

These celestial vanishings,
these drowned continents,

the lightning fields flashing
all night long in the rain.

3   Whose grief is this, wild haired,
singing, in the wind?

Chokecherry blossoms,
canker worms, rustling prairie grass.

The gorgeous eye of the dead deer,
iridescent, terrible.

In the desert I heard
stones weeping.

Every breath, every pulse,
every shiver rippling out, forever.

In every cave a gypsy.
Our embroidered dead, O beloved.

4   These dozen hooded faces
empty, hollow, turned to the sun.

Arthritic symptoms
could mean: mineral deficiencies,

deer ticks, genetic weaknesses,
accumulated steroids,

unexpressed rage.
So many empty gin bottles

behind the red woodshed.
So much depends upon.

Signs and wonders,
earth grommets in the fields.

5   Shall we harness the stones,
verily, bind them with steel?

The blackbirds are angry:
give them back their seeds.

We who have lived without
hope, these long centuries,

can we survive one more winter?
Mice huddled in tree roots,

hawk's shadow.
Goose down, bilberries,

hot lava. Brandy
in small glasses, *na zdravje.*

6   Tell the doctors:
no more chemotherapies!

All our rivers and lakes now glow
in the dark.

SK8 duking it out with the partisans,
Darth Vader spidering

through the medieval town square
of pink roofed Maribor.

Trout leaping from the river Drava
into the fishermen's hands.

Blond boys, insistent: so many
innocent ex-communists to exploit.

7   What was it we wanted,
     before all the walls came down?

     Blue grey eyes, looking at me,
     through the cigarette smoke.

     Heil Mister Herr Direktor Daddy
     Doktor Präsident CEO Sir!

     That is no country for old women,
     every oak slashed from root to crown.

     The children breathing in
     the by-products of petroleum.

     Vineyards gleaming,
     fruitladen, on the sun drenched hills.

8   Let us have more mastectomies,
     cut them all off!

     Once out of nature we can sing
     all the louder, n'est-ce pas,

     ma soeur, mon semblable?
     The disobedient cells vanquished,

     a clean nation without breasts,
     once and for all.

     Flat-chested mothers renouncing
     their children in the public baths.

     The poets ranting beautifully
     in the dark, drunk on stolen wine.

9   So many newly minted young
capitalists on the make.

The golden rule:
self sacrifice, or suicide.

The curve of the sweet earth,
herb scented, holy.

Bring them along, these crotch sniffers,
these bags of fur,

squirrel chasers, diggers of corpses,
rollers in horse dung.

Rotted fish on the world's beaches,
jewelled with black flies, beetles.

10   Now that it's much much too late,
now you care.

Poison ivy wrapped around the
ash trees; lover's embrace.

Turtle, are you crazy, get
your diamond shell off the damn road.

The eating and the eaten, all
are gathered here, dearly beloved.

The blood, the liver, remember
our mother tongues.

A species gone every three minutes.
History racing us by.

11   Thank you Chrysler for this squashed
gopher blood bug feast amen.

I touch the earth, the earth touches me.
I feel the earth, the earth feels me.

Twenty-five billion Barbies,
plastic harems for everyone.

The yard hungry for rust, seducing
dead cars in the rain.

Each of us flaunting our
skeletons in front of the Opera Café,

elbows flying, eyes in the trees.
Fire-fangled feathers dangling down.

12   Crowds pacing at the entrances
to the realms of the dead.

Thing One and Thing Two
in boots and black leather:

It was you, no it was you.
You you you you you you you.

Dancing under red electric light
to Mozart's *Requiem*.

How much did you have to bribe
the ferryman?

Guarding the gate for your beloveds.
Well, what would you do?

✳

after Donna Haraway

Not ungrateful for the attempt at proper
institutionalization, Mr. Vice President,
those twenty piece place settings inside
your walls, though it is you with your
head in the clouds, engineering our wild
minds with your long armed industrial
screws and custom made hard wired hat,
your poems locked in secret drawers,
invisible you thought, but we have x-ray
eyes, all our night flying has made us
bold, here we come riding quantumly
through your armoured glass windows
on our multicoloured cyborged wings,
still bats, witches, goddesses, still unruly
mistresses of our, your, the world's pulsing
heart

Afterword

You pray for the rare flower to appear

I grew up in Reinland, a tiny traditionalist Mennonite village in southern Manitoba, in the middle of the gorgeous wide sky flat flat prairie, surrounded by several dozen other villages much like ours, with beautiful German flower names, Rosengart, Blumenfeld, Schönwiese. I thought, growing up, the whole world was just like that, small villages filled with singing and laughter (and also griefs of all sizes), intricate extended family networks that encompassed numerous villages, and a wonderful wild rugged landscape we pitted our energetic human labours against, in order to wrestle from it a rich but humble living, intimate, communal, plain style, close to the ground.

We did not think of ourselves as a "minority" culture, we did not understand ourselves as "ethnic" or "immigrant" or "multicultural." We were an ancient stubborn peasant people who had refused modernization and assimilation to print culture, and the rise of the nation state, during the industrial revolution and after. Our ancestors had paid a very high price for our cultural independence, suffering large scale extermination during the Burning Times, and exile and recurring political persecutions in several countries, in inhospitable landscapes, before landing gratefully in relatively peaceful Canada in the late 1800s. We identified ambivalently with the First Nations people of North America whose tragic displacements had enabled our arrival. We did not consider ourselves Canadian; we were a tribal people, our identity was firmly embedded in our communal stories and peasant traditions, in songs and rituals. We used Christian language in our formal meetings, but it was an overlay on a much older, more pagan, irreverent, comic, bawdy sensibility, which we preserved in the daily mode through various folk rituals and our dialect, *Plautdietsch*. We felt very close to the land, but we did not consider it ours in any permanent sense. We were resolutely pacifist, and antimodernist, willing to remain migrant in order to preserve our old village ways; our suitcases stood ready, always, near the door.

The Manitoba Compulsory Education Act of 1919, which required all Manitoba children to attend public school, with a British-centred English curriculum, strictly enforced through closure of alternative schools, was a fraught event for the Manitoba Mennonites, many of whom fled to less governmentally controlled landscapes, primarily in Mexico and Central and South America. Those of us who stayed wrestled with the effects of a modern English education, and the children of my generation, who were the first to have access to public school and university educations en masse, suffered intense intergenerational conflicts as we gradually, inevitably, began to assimilate to the world around us, and to relax the tight hold of our martyr-inflected identity.

I spent my adolescence and young adulthood trying to get as far away from this "backwards," beleaguered heritage as possible. Becoming a professionally published poet was, as I understood from the beginning, a treasonous act. I betrayed every linguistic rule and convention that held our communal identity tightly and increasingly precariously together. Orality is impossible to preserve in a situation of modern book and media education. Preserving ancient peasant ways is impossible in a post-industrial context. It's possible to champion the wrong parts as the heritage slips, wounded, from your grasp. In any case we had already become hybrid, had indeed always been uncomfortably hybrid, at least since the time of our exile, buying into certain aspects of modernization and patriarchal hierarchalism, while fiercely guarding our communal, egalitarian peasant sensibilities in selected areas. Unfortunately, in my view, the Mennonites of Canada were susceptible to American evangelical Christian fundamentalist influence in the vulnerable moment of beginning to speak English, timidly entering into print and radio culture at last, in the 1940s and '50s. The children of my generation were susceptible to cultural shame as we began to understand and internalize mainstream Canadian views about our traditionalist independence.

I'm not sure to what extent that old ecstatic visionary world, marvelously preserved in the villages right into the 1950s, the years of my childhood, still exists: very little, according to Miriam Toews's celebrated novel, *A Complicated Kindness* (Stoddart 2004). Conservationism mixed with fear morphs easily into conservatism (just as innovation, in the modern paradigm, easily turns into destructiveness). The internal contradictions in the cultural codes of the community by the time I came along were enough to make a sensitive thinking person crazy! This is not the story of one woman, one family, one minority culture alone; it is the story of many of the world's peoples, around the globe.

I am talking about my lost heritage, unmistakably rooted in ancient, wild minded, indigenous ways of being, greatly mourned by me despite my reluctant but ultimately willing betrayal of it, my extended battle with every spirit restricting aspect of it, to make the case that writing poetry has been, for me, despite the angry rejection of it in my home community (resulting in various degrees of shunning for both me and my daughters), as close a way of recuperating the ecstatic, oracular, celebratory, mythopoeic, magical sense of language and deep feeling sensibility I grew up with, as I could possibly come to, in the often bewildering cross-cultural context of modern Canada that has been the rest of my life. Like a bird on a wire, ah, indeed, like a drunk in a midnight choir, I have tried, in my way, to be true.

Language, in the postmodern sense, holds so much less power and efficacy than that old prophetic, visionary, metaphoric language, which encompassed earth and sky, and every imaginable realm of existence between hell and heaven. Speaking words, naming the world, especially in a public context, was an act of power, of creation, of establishing relation, within the range of the divine. We were practical, materialist, satirical, comedic, but we were also dreamers, seers, bards. We did not choose between flesh and spirit, fact and myth, eros and divinity, reason and feeling, human and natural, earthly and cosmic, as people nowadays seem forced to do. Miracles and shapeshifting rebirths, transformations, were easily within the realm of our expectations. All these dimensions were eloquently and elegantly woven together in our activities and rituals, our daily encounter with animals and the living land, our sermons, our poetry, our singing.

Much of my poetics derives, despite my defection from the traditional ways, from the village practices of singing folk songs and hymns, all day, every day, during milking, picking strawberries, cutting the hay: a kind of joyful praise of the gorgeous living world, turning often on ceremonial occasions to high grief, at the mortality running through everything, the temporariness of our brief tenure on this earth, the loss of our beloveds, our homelands, the necessity of hunger, of having to eat, the ravages of winter, the brown edge of the green leaf. Rhythm as the great consolation, the healing salve, in a world seared through with loss, the intimate pleasure of the singing voice, its connective vibrations, its porous resonances, a sounding deep in our bones, our cells, the heart's cry, the desire that drives us, the pleasure that throbs in us, a thriving we hold in common with other species after all, and perhaps with the fabric of life itself, the structural DNA, the energetic quaver at the centre of the molecule, the song of the cicadas, thrumming bees, the rustle of trees, howl of coyotes, gurgling rivers, sway of wildflowers in the wind, imperceptible breathing of rocks, underground shift of tectonic plates, chorus of glaciers, whispering grass.

It is the great irony of modernity, that the huge increases in wealth and technological power and mobility and speed in the so-called developed world, which have given us capabilities of travel and information and large-scale interventions of every sort, on a scale never before dreamed of, have been accompanied by the steady impoverishment of our poetic and spiritual lives, and the gradual narrowing of our senses, our intuition, our singing souls. The price of technologization has been tragically high, in its destruction of local cultures and rituals of ecstasy, in its ruthless exploitation of natural landscapes, animals and ecosystems: here we are heading into global eco-crisis with our diminished immune systems and enfeebled imaginations and hearing/feeling loss, and not enough contingency plans in sight.

Now that the prosthetic, inflationary, wîhtiko logic of modernity is running out, traditionalist knowledges don't seem so backward anymore, with their fantastic visionary capacities and local, playful, humble, environmental engagements and rituals of caring. As Martín Prechtel has observed, there are still "spiritually intact" cultures on the earth, in which the extravagant relational logic of poetry prevails over modern discourses of alienation and domination. Medéllin, Columbia, is the site of one such culture, where poetry is profoundly understood and cherished by people of all ages, in the mainstream arena, from young to old, as I was lucky enough to witness and experience recently. (Is it accidental, or indeed surprising, in the history of Western culture, that this sensitive, deep feeling, tender people should be so hounded by spectres of violence, a scene of intense internationally fuelled contestations over its affiliations and spiritual loyalties?)

We in the so-called developed countries have nearly forgotten what poetry is, what it is for, so marginalized has it become as a public discourse. And yet it has shown remarkable resilience, for all that, holding stubbornly on to its irrational surreal playful metaphoric intuitive transformative relational capacities, born around ancient ritual fires and still miraculously au courant, post printing press, post typewriter, flourishing in the electronic media, and nudging playfully, tenderly, erotically, heroically, passionately, against mainstream contemporary discourses, which are infused now, despite or because of their strict emphasis on rationalist analysis and individual freedom, with genetic determinism and paranoia and militarisms. *Mind itself is Magic coursing through the flesh, and flesh itself is Magic dancing on a clock, and time itself the Magic Length of God.* It is not surprising that Leonard Cohen and Buffy Sainte-Marie, shaking off similar histories of cultural persecution by the Western mainstream, and rising up to sing eloquently about their reparation, should have been such inspiring and influential poetic models for me.

I am grateful to have come to poetry in a time when the spirits of experimentalism and postcolonialism and feminism were at a height in Canada, in the 1980s, a hundred years after my ancestors arrived on this continent, frightened, destitute, garrisoned. I am grateful to have come to it in a time of relative peace and prosperity, where I could risk asking forbidden questions without being killed for it (though it has not been easy, I have feared for my life at times for my temerity). It has been a moment of great historic privilege, of thawing out, of returning to the site of trauma and exile that marked the beginning of the long migrancy of my people from one country to another, and reconnecting with the larger world. I am grateful to all the great teachers and mentors and colleagues and friends who have helped make it so. I am happy to be able to claim a much broader range of cultural affiliations than the narrow one I grew up with.

I am grateful to have come to poetry as a woman and as a mother, joyfully connected to the reproductive rhythms of the living earth, fearfully awakened to the possibilities of the future, the environmental dangers we now face on a global scale. The heroic maternal practice of intimate, daily caring of growing children, with very little social support, while at the same time competing with less-encumbered colleagues in the professional arena, taught me strength and courage to wrestle with the pervasive despair of our time, to reach beyond the fashionable postmodern stances of irony and exposé and shared narcissisms toward more intersubjective, recreative, reparative strategies to confront the daunting challenges of our age.

There is a mystery at the heart of poetry: people want to know the recipe, but there is none. There is what Don McKay calls "poetic attention," to the beauty and ugliness, joy and suffering, of everything around you, there is the heightened attentiveness to sound, rhythm, image, breath, spacing. The grand struggle with form, the impossible leap between the blood, the wild heart, rooted in primitive, fantastic memories and sensations and dreams and desires, and the page in front of you, the here and now, the material world in front of you, the solid or rickety stage you stand on.

There are many schools of brilliant tricks to sharpen your formal skills, imagism, surrealism, decadence, vorticism, to name a few that have been important to me, projective verse, dada, sound, dub, transelation, rewriting of old forms, ghazals, ballads, hymns, psalms, prose poetry, science poetry, l=a=n=g=u=a=g=e, oulipo. You can never get it right, the form resists you, has a mind, a will of its own. So do the muses, redoubtable mistresses, whispering naughty things in your ear, insistent. It's hard to imagine, sometimes, in this poetically bereft culture, who the audience will be, you have to call it up out of nowhere, energetically, and hope some real people will join you there. There is the ubiquitous problem of the subject, who is speaking, what are we speaking about, and for: "Who is this I infesting my poems?" writes Phyllis Webb. "Can poetry alone exist in isolation from,*" asks Erin Mouré, and footnotes the line with "*'where' the car slowed (bitch, he said)." Or, as Christopher Dewdney offers, sidestepping ego but not desire, "The associational areola is contiguous with surrounding areolas such that the 'nipples' are adrift in an areolar ocean." This is where the poetic labour is, the negotiation between numerous clamouring forces and resistances, sometimes it's an exhausting tournament, a battle, a tease, a torment, sometimes it's a dance, fluid, fiery, chemicals leaping, sparks in the air. Auras of light around the trees. Evolutionary. Alchemical.

It's a great poetic exercise to imitate the poets you admire, worship their spirits, absorb their techniques. Here are some of mine, in no particular order: Leonard Cohen, John Thompson, Phyllis Webb, Dorothy Livesay, Margaret Atwood, Sylvia Plath, René Char, Sappho, Robert Kroetsch, Martín Prechtel, Michael Ondaatje, Mari-Lou Rowley, Louise (Sky Dancer) Halfe, Libby Scheier, Lillian Allen, Hélène Cixous, Paul Célan, Rainer Maria Rilke, Johann Wolfgang von Goethe, William Blake, William Wordsworth, Christopher Dewdney, Christian Bök, bpNichol, Patrick Friesen, Mahmoud Darwish, Wallace Stevens, T.S. Eliot, H.D., William Butler Yeats, Daphne Marlatt, Erin Mouré.

My greatest formal struggle has been how to contain a very very long breath line (an old Germanic oral cadence that comes naturally to me) on the page, in a way that's manageable to modern eyes and ears. Sometimes I let the line run on wildly, punctuationless, with arbitrary wide margins, proliferating resonances in all directions, sometimes I tighten it up, like a guitar string, as tight as it will go, and force it into enjambment. Sometimes I calm it down into thin couplets, flattening the resonances, for the sake of resisting embedded metaphors. Sometimes I line up the line at the left margin, harshly, Sir! with capital letters and commas and periods: barefoot prairie grrrl on the 401 dons helmet and steel toed boots. I work hard at slowing the pace of the line, for the sake of the poor breathless reader/listener, but as soon as I relax vigilance, off it gallops again.

It's great to compare notes with poetic companions, preferably over drinks! to cry and laugh with them over the paradoxes of the poetic life, its waywardness, fragility, resilience, strength. *Ne zdravje!* But then there is the part where you must go it alone, no one can show you, no one knows. You can't force it to happen, you prepare the soil for it, you gesso the canvas, you paint the tree, you pray for the rare flower to appear, lightning to spark, the never before seen beautiful shining bird to alight on its branches. It is a gift, it is a calling, it is available to everyone, accomplished only by a few.

We are entering a new era, in which the certainties of the modern are crumbling. The petroleum is running out. The weather is out of whack. The pandemic is on its way. Television, the new media hope of postmodernism, has degenerated into commercial and government propaganda. Somewhere, in the fear and trembling that mark our anticipation of the not yet known just around the corner, a new mode of being in the world, a new imaginative paradigm, is being formed. Yeats, nearly a hundred years ago, foresaw mass violence for his century, and proposed an artificial bird in a golden cage as an answer to the uncertainties of history and the volatility of the blood. We, teetering on the brink of political and environmental apocalypse, have the challenge and possibility of imagining the future of our planet in radically revisionary ways, past the despair that marks our historical moment, with its heritage of mass violence and overcultivation of natural processes, grieving its false optimisms, opening ourselves to new beginnings in the midst of grand endings: rediscovering the interconnectedness of everything, the green world recovering its strength, language remembering its life giving power, our spirits singing in chorus with the breathing world, uncaged, not above it, not against it, our blood pulsing in harmony with its rhythms, deep rooted, poetically.

—Di Brandt

Acknowledgements

From *questions i asked my mother*
Winnipeg: Turnstone, 1987
> when i was five i thought heaven was located
> but what do you think my father says this verse means if it's not
> say to yourself each time lips vagina tongue
> my mother found herself one late summer
> missionary position (1)
> missionary position (5)
> mother why didn't you tell me this

From *Agnes in the sky*
Winnipeg: Turnstone, 1990
> you prepare a banquet in your mind
> since we cannot meet on father ground
> nonresistance, or love Mennonite style
> prairie hymn

From *mother, not mother*
Toronto: Mercury, 1992
> why she can't write *the mother*
> let me tell you, dear reader
> completely seduced
> what *de Englische*
> the letters i wrote & didn't
> poem for a guy who's
> death is a good argument
> today i spit out God & Jesus

From *Jerusalem, beloved*
Winnipeg: Turnstone, 1995
> & it amuses us to think that in death you're becoming
> Jerusalem, the golden, city of my dreams

there are no words in me for Gaza, for what i saw
how long does it take to forget a murder in your
here, in the desert, where everything comes together
how badly she wants peace, this wise woman, this

From *Now You Care*
Toronto: Coach House, 2003
      Zone: < le Détroit > 1
      Zone: < le Détroit > 2
      Here at the heart of the ravaged heart
      Dog days in Maribor: Anti (electric) ghazals
      Not ungrateful for the attempt at proper

July 17/09 TPL